SAFETY BUTTON POPS UP WHEN
ORIGINAL SEAL IS BROKEN

SAFETY
BUTTON

Snapple

To:

D1559255

From:

BUTTON POPS UP WHEN
ORIGINAL SEAL IS BROKEN

Snapple

POPS
UP

BUTTON IS UP

Snapple

Snapple

POPS
UP

REJECT IF BUTTON IS UP

REJECT IF BUTTON IS UP

Snapple

Real facts ™

PETER PAUPER PRESS, INC.
White Plains, New York

For more Snapple Real Facts,
visit us at www. snapple.com

Designed by Taryn R. Sefecka

Published by:
Peter Pauper Press, Inc.
202 Mamaroneck Avenue
White Plains, NY 10601
All rights reserved
ISBN 978-0-88088-582-9
Printed in China
14   13   12   11   10   9

Visit us at www.peterpauper.com

real fact # 137

- The city of Los Angeles has 3x more automobiles than people.

real fact # 116

- The largest fish is the whale shark–it can be over 50 feet long and weigh 2 tons.

real fact # 163

- The first penny had the motto "Mind your own business."

real fact # 222

• "Twinkle Twinkle Little Star" was composed by Mozart when he was five years old.

real fact # 196

• If you doubled one penny every day for 30 days, you would have $5,368,709.12.

real fact # 156

• Swimming pools in the U.S. contain enough water to cover San Francisco.

Mosquitoes are attracted to people who have recently eaten bananas.

A stamp shaped like a banana was once issued in the country of Tonga.

The Basenji is the only type of dog that does not bark.

SAFETY BUTTON POPS UP WHEN ORIGINAL SEAL IS BROKEN

SAFETY BUTTON

Snapple

P.O.'S '11

REJECT IF BUTTON IS UP

"Real Fact" # 207

Before 1687 clocks were made with only an hour hand.

Get all the "Real Facts" at snapple.com

"Real Fact" # 54

The average smell weighs 760 nanograms.

Get all the "Real Facts" at snapple.com

real fact # 164

- The first vacuum was so large, it was brought to a house with horses.

real fact # 106

- You would weigh less on the top of a mountain than at sea level.

real fact # 205

- For every human being in the world there is approximately one chicken.

real fact # 28

- Chewing gum while peeling onions will keep you from crying.

real fact # 213

- The largest ball of twine in the U.S. weighs over 17,000 pounds.

The hummingbird
is the only bird
that can fly
backwards.

A hummingbird's
heart beats fourteen
hundred times a minute.

A hummingbird
weighs less than a penny.

"Real Fact" # 103

Frowning burns more calories than smiling.

Get all the "Real Facts" at snapple.com

"Real Fact" # 124

Seals sleep only one and a half minutes at a time.

Get all the "Real Facts" at snapple.com

SAFETY BUTTON POPS UP WHEN ORIGINAL SEAL IS BROKEN

SAFETY BUTTON

Snapple®

POPS UP

REJECT IF BUTTON IS UP

"Real Fact" # 36

A duck's quack doesn't echo.

Get all the "Real Facts" at snapple.com

real fact # 165
- Your eye expands up to 45% when looking at something pleasing.

real fact # 171
- The most sensitive parts of the body are the mouth and the fingertips.

real fact # 53
- The average woman consumes 6 pounds of lipstick in her lifetime.

real fact # 34

- If you keep a goldfish in a dark room, it will eventually turn white.

real fact # 197

- The first person crossed Niagara Falls by tightrope in 1859.

real fact # 75

- The average person makes 1,140 phone calls each year.

real fact # 109

Smelling bananas and/or apples can help you lose weight.

real fact # 175

In 1634, tulip bulbs were a form of currency in Holland.

real fact # 74

You share your birthday with at least a million other people.

real fact # 46

Elephants are the only mammals that can't jump.

"Real Fact" # 79

There are 119 grooves on the edge of a quarter.

Get all the "Real Facts" at snapple.com

SAFETY BUTTON POPS UP WHEN ORIGINAL SEAL IS BROKEN

SAFETY BUTTON

Snapple

POP'S UP

REJECT IF BUTTON IS UP

"Real Fact" # 60

The tongue is the fastest healing part of a human body.

Get all the "Real Facts" at snapple.com

real fact # 57

- You blink over 10,000,000 times a year.

real fact # 105

- You will burn about 7% more calories walking on hard dirt than pavement.

real fact # 173

- Chinese is the most spoken language in the world.

real fact # 143

- "Q" is the only letter in the alphabet not appearing in the name of any U.S. state.

real fact # 225

- There are towns named Sandwich in Illinois and Massachusetts.

real fact # 11

flamingos turn pink from eating shrimp.

real fact # 69

No word in the English language rhymes with month.

There are 18 different animal shapes in the animal crackers cookie zoo.

The fastest recorded speed of a racehorse was over 43 mph.

"Real Fact" # 24

The State of Maine has 62 lighthouses.

Get all the "Real Facts" at snapple.com

SAFETY BUTTON POPS UP WHEN ORIGINAL SEAL IS BROKEN

SAFETY BUTTON

Snapple

REJECT IF BUTTON IS UP

"Real Fact" # 66

Americans on average eat 18 acres of pizza every day.

Get all the "Real Facts" at snapple.com

"Real Fact" # 218

A jackrabbit can travel more than 12 feet in one hop.

Get all the "Real Facts" at snapple.com

"Real Fact" # 209

The largest pumpkin ever grown weighed 1,061 lbs.

Get all the "Real Facts" at snapple.com

SAFETY BUTTON POPS UP WHEN ORIGINAL SEAL IS BROKEN

SAFETY BUTTON

Snapple®

POP!

REJECT IF BUTTON IS UP

"Real Fact" # 47

Giraffes have no vocal cords.

Get all the "Real Facts" at snapple.com

real fact # 22

- Alaska has the highest percentage of people who walk to work.

real fact # 176

- The first bike was called a hobbyhorse.

real fact # 167

- You have to play ping-pong for 12 hours to lose one pound.

real fact # 144

- Texas is the only state that permits residents to cast absentee ballots from space.

real fact # 29

- On average, a human being will spend up to 2 weeks kissing in his/her lifetime.

real fact # 180

- The first VCR was made in 1956 and was the size of a piano.

real fact # 42

frogs cannot swallow with their eyes open.

real fact # 44

The bullfrog is the only animal that never sleeps.

A single coffee tree produces only about a pound of coffee beans per year.

Hawaii is the only U.S. state that grows coffee.

SAFETY BUTTON POPS UP WHEN ORIGINAL SEAL IS BROKEN

SAFETY BUTTON

Snapple

REJECT IF BUTTON IS UP

"Real Fact" # 4

Slugs have
4 noses.

Get all the "Real Facts" at snapple.com

"Real Fact" # 70

A "jiffy" is 1/100
of a second.

Get all the "Real Facts" at snapple.com

"Real Fact" # 90

The average
raindrop falls at 7
miles per hour.

Get all the "Real Facts" at snapple.com

"Real Fact" # 140

Holland is the only country with a national dog.

Get all the "Real Facts" at snapple.com

"Real Fact" # 88

A ten gallon hat holds less than one gallon of liquid.

Get all the "Real Facts" at snapple.com

SAFETY BUTTON POPS UP WHEN ORIGINAL SEAL IS BROKEN

SAFETY BUTTON

Snapple

POP'S UP

REJECT IF BUTTON IS UP

real fact # 194
- You don't have to be a lawyer to be a Supreme Court Justice.

real fact # 157
- The first TV soap opera debuted in 1946.

real fact # 146

- The smallest county in America is New York County, better known as Manhattan.

real fact # 160

- One alternate title that had been considered for NBC's hit "Friends" was "Insomnia Cafe."

real fact # 111

- Only male turkeys gobble.

real fact # 228

There is a town in South Dakota named "Tea."

real fact # 226

13 percent of the world's tea comes from Kenya.

real fact # 227

"Tsiology" is anything written about tea.

real fact # 86

Until the nineteenth century, solid blocks of tea were used as money in Siberia.

"Real Fact" # 190

Thailand means
"Land of the Free."

Get all the "Real Facts" at snapple.com

"Real Fact" # 26

The Hawaiian
alphabet has only
12 letters.

Get all the "Real Facts" at snapple.com

SAFETY BUTTON POPS UP WHEN
ORIGINAL SEAL IS BROKEN

SAFETY BUTTON

Snapple

REJECT IF BUTTON IS UP

"Real Fact" # 139

Hawaii is the only
state with one
school district.

Get all the "Real Facts" at snapple.com

real fact # 155

- In 1926, the first outdoor mini-golf courses were built on rooftops in NYC.

real fact # 58

- A sneeze travels out of your mouth at over 100 miles per hour.

real fact # 65

- A one-day weather forecast requires about 10 billion mathematical calculations.

real fact # 73

- The average person spends 2 weeks over his/her life waiting for a traffic light to change.

real fact # 133

- Honeybees navigate by using the sun as a compass.

real fact # 49

- Despite its hump, a camel has a straight spine.

11% of the people in the world are left-handed.

Add up opposing sides of a dice cube and you'll always get seven.

When the moon is
directly overhead,
you weigh less.

1/4 of the
bones in your body
are in your feet.

SAFETY BUTTON POPS UP WHEN ORIGINAL SEAL IS BROKEN

SAFETY BUTTON

Snapple

POP'S

REJECT IF BUTTON IS UP

"Real Fact" # 217

Blackboard chalk contains no chalk.

Get all the "Real Facts" at snapple.com

"Real Fact" # 83

Googol is a number (1 followed by 100 zeros).

Get all the "Real Facts" at snapple.com

"Real Fact" # 215

Tennessee banned the use of a lasso to catch fish.

Get all the "Real Facts" at snapple.com

"Real Fact" #6

A honey bee can fly at 15 miles per hour.

Get all the "Real Facts" at snapple.com

SAFETY BUTTON POPS UP WHEN ORIGINAL SEAL IS BROKEN

SAFETY BUTTON

POP'S UP

Snapple

REJECT IF BUTTON IS UP

"Real Fact" #177

The first sailing boats were built in Egypt.

Get all the "Real Facts" at snapple.com

real fact # 149
- Theodore Roosevelt was the only president blind in one eye.

real fact # 114
- The oldest known animal was a tortoise and lived to be 152 years old.

real fact # 224

- America's 1st roller coaster was built in 1827 to carry coal from a mine to boats below.

real fact # 32

- There are 1 million ants for every human in the world.

real fact # 117

- The starfish is the only animal that can turn its stomach inside out.

real fact # 21

Almonds are members of the peach family.

real fact # 221

The game of basketball was first played using a soccer ball and two peach baskets.

The average American will eat 35,000 cookies during his/her lifetime.

1.3 billion pounds of peanuts are produced in Georgia each year.

"Real Fact" # 148

The tallest man
was 8 ft. 11 in.

Get all the "Real Facts" at snapple.com

SAFETY BUTTON POPS UP WHEN
ORIGINAL SEAL IS BROKEN

SAFETY
BUTTON

Snapple ®

POPS
UP

REJECT IF BUTTON IS UP

"Real Fact" # 93

A kangaroo can
jump 30 feet.

Get all the "Real Facts" at snapple.com

"Real Fact" # 150

The first sport
to be filmed was
boxing in 1894.

Get all the "Real Facts" at snapple.com

"Real Fact" # 13

Cats have over
one hundred
vocal cords.

Get all the "Real Facts" at snapple.com

SAFETY BUTTON POPS UP WHEN
ORIGINAL SEAL IS BROKEN

SAFETY
BUTTON

Snapple®

REJECT IF BUTTON IS UP

"Real Fact" # 7

A queen bee can
lay 800–1,500
eggs per day.

Get all the "Real Facts" at snapple.com

real fact # 120

- The only continent without reptiles or snakes is Antarctica.

real fact # 100

- In a year, the average person walks four miles making his or her bed.

real fact # 151

- The fastest served ball in tennis was clocked at 154 miles per hour in 1963.

real fact # 20

- Broccoli and Cauliflower are the only vegetables that are flowers.

real fact # 168

- One brow wrinkle is the result of 200,000 frowns.

real fact # 131

- Penguins have an organ above their eyes that converts seawater to freshwater.

The year that read the same upside down was 1961. That won't happen again until 6009.

Mosquitoes have 47 teeth.

Hawaii is the only
U.S. state never to
report a temperature
of zero.

Giraffes can
lick their own eyes.

"Real Fact" # 101

About half of all Americans are on a diet on any given day.

Get all the "Real Facts" at snapple.com

"Real Fact" # 201

The only single–syllable U.S. state is Maine.

Get all the "Real Facts" at snapple.com

SAFETY BUTTON POPS UP WHEN ORIGINAL SEAL IS BROKEN

SAFETY BUTTON

Snapple

POPS UP

REJECT IF BUTTON IS UP

real fact # 183

- The Capitol building in Washington, DC has 365 steps to represent every day of the year.

real fact # 178

- The first ballpoint pens were sold in 1945 for $12.00.

real fact # 192

- Jupiter spins so fast that there is a new sunrise nearly every ten hours.

real fact # 40

- It is possible to lead a cow up stairs but not down stairs.

real fact # 63

- The average human produces 10,000 gallons of saliva in a lifetime.

real fact # 64

Strawberries contain more Vitamin C than oranges.

real fact # 136

Strawberries are the only fruit whose seeds grow on the outside.

A crocodile cannot move its tongue.

The first TV show ever to be put into reruns was "The Lone Ranger."

"Real Fact" # 15

All porcupines
float in water.

Get all the "Real Facts" at snapple.com

SAFETY BUTTON POPS UP WHEN
ORIGINAL SEAL IS BROKEN

SAFETY
BUTTON

Snapple®

PUSH
UP

REJECT IF BUTTON IS UP

"Real Fact" # 152

In 1985, the
fastest bicyclist
was clocked at
154 mph.

Get all the "Real Facts" at snapple.com

"Real Fact" # 81

Alaska has more caribou than people.

Get all the "Real Facts" at snapple.com

"Real Fact" # 107

You burn more calories sleeping than you do watching t.v.

Get all the "Real Facts" at snapple.com

"Real Fact" # 128

Dragonflies have six legs but cannot walk.

Get all the "Real Facts" at snapple.com

SAFETY BUTTON POPS UP WHEN ORIGINAL SEAL IS BROKEN

SAFETY BUTTON

Snapple®

POPS UP

REJECT IF BUTTON IS UP

real fact # 23
- The San Francisco cable cars are the only mobile national monuments.

real fact # 170
- In 1878, the first telephone book ever issued contained only 50 names.

real fact # 172
- The eye makes movements 50 times every second.

real fact # 84

- Oysters can change from one gender to another and back again.

real fact # 179

- The first lighthouse to use electricity was the Statue of Liberty in 1886.

real fact # 125

- Pigeons have been trained by the U.S. Coast Guard to spot people lost at sea.

real fact # 158

The first MTV video was "Video Killed the Radio Star," by the Buggles.

real fact # 220

Porcupines each have 30,000 quills.

No piece of paper
can be folded in half
more than 7 times.

The mouth of
the Statue of
Liberty is 3 feet wide.

SAFETY BUTTON POPS UP WHEN
ORIGINAL SEAL IS BROKEN

SAFETY
BUTTON

Snapple ®

POPS
UP

REJECT IF BUTTON IS UP

"Real Fact" # 19

Children grow
faster in
the spring.

Get all the "Real Facts" at snapple.com

"Real Fact" # 85

The Mona Lisa
has no eyebrows.

Get all the "Real Facts" at snapple.com

"Real Fact" # 55

A human brain
weighs about
3 lbs.

Get all the "Real Facts" at snapple.com

SAFETY BUTTON POPS UP WHEN
ORIGINAL SEAL IS BROKEN

SAFETY
BUTTON

Snapple

POP'S
UP

REJECT IF BUTTON IS UP

"Real Fact" # 92

Fish can drown.

Get all the "Real Facts" at snapple.com

"Real Fact" # 82

August has
the highest
percentages
of births.

Get all the "Real Facts" at snapple.com

real fact # 3

• Beavers can hold their breath for 45 minutes.

real fact # 154

• Americans spend more than $630 million a year on golf balls.

real fact # 91

- There are more telephones than people in Washington, D.C.

real fact # 195

- Eleven of the fifty U.S. states are named after an actual person.

real fact # 141

- The square dance is the official dance of the state of Washington.

real fact # 130

Koalas and
humans are the
only animals
with unique
fingerprints.

The average
koala sleeps 22 hours
each day.

Bamboo makes
up 99% of a panda's diet.

"Real Fact" # 99

You burn 20 calories per hour chewing gum.

Get all the "Real Facts" at snapple.com

SAFETY BUTTON POPS UP WHEN ORIGINAL SEAL IS BROKEN

SAFETY BUTTON

Snapple®

REJECT IF BUTTON IS UP

"Real Fact" # 25

The only food that doesn't spoil is honey.

Get all the "Real Facts" at snapple.com

"Real Fact" # 37

A snail breathes through its foot.

Get all the "Real Facts" at snapple.com

"Real Fact" # 102

A one-minute kiss burns 26 calories.

Get all the "Real Facts" at snapple.com

SAFETY BUTTON POPS UP WHEN ORIGINAL SEAL IS BROKEN

SAFETY BUTTON

Snapple®

POPS UP

REJECT IF BUTTON IS UP

"Real Fact" # 199

The largest cheese ever made weighed 57,508 lbs.

Get all the "Real Facts" at snapple.com

real fact # 31

- The average human eats 8 spiders in his/her lifetime while sleeping.

real fact # 121

- The only bird that can swim but not fly is the penguin.

real fact # 12

- Emus and kangaroos cannot walk backwards.

real fact # 72
- The average person uses 150 gallons of water a day for personal use.

real fact # 76
- The average person spends about 2 years on the phone in a lifetime.

real fact # 27
- A ball of glass will bounce higher than a ball of rubber.

SAFETY BUTTON POPS UP WHEN ORIGINAL SEAL IS BROKEN
SAFETY BUTTON
Snapple
POPS UP
REJECT IF BUTTON IS UP
SAFETY BUTTON POPS UP WHEN ORIGINAL SEAL IS BROKEN
diet Snapple
REJECT IF BUTTON IS UP